Sumana the Novice Monk

©2015 All Rights Reserved

ISBN: 978-955-0614-78-3

Computer Typesetting by

Mahamevnawa Buddhist Monastery, Toronto
Markham, Ontario, Canada L6C 1P2
Telephone: 905-927-7117
www.mahamevnawa.ca

Published by

Mahamegha Publishers
Waduwawa, Yatigaloluwa, Polgahawela, Sri Lanka.
Telephone: +94 37 2053300 | 77 3216685
www.mahameghapublishers.com
mahameghapublishers@gmail.com

Sumana the Novice Monk

*With the guidance and direction of
Most Venerable Kiribathgoda Gnānānanda Thera*

Artwork by Sumathipāla & Jothipāla

A Mahamegha Publication

Sumana the Novice Monk

My dear children,

The trainee monk-Samanera, Sumana received ordination under Arahath Anuruddha when he was only seven years old. In preparation for monkhood, his hair was shaved off. And at that very same time he was most fortunate to attain the Supreme Bliss of Nibbāna and become a great Arahath.

A few days after becoming a monk, young Arahath Sumana and Arahath Anuruddha went to see the Supreme Buddha, who was staying at a monastery in a forest near the Himalaya Mountains. Using their special powers they both travelled through the air. However, during those days Arahath Anuruddha was suffering from a stomach ailment.

"Bhante, it looks like you're in a lot of pain. Are you feeling sick?" asked Samanera Sumana from Arahath Anuruddha. "Yes, Sumana, I am suffering from a stomach ailment. That's what's causing all this pain," said Arahath Anuruddha. Then, Samanera Sumana asked, "Bhante, do you know what kind of medication would help you get well?" "Drinking some water from Lake Anavatapta will help me recover," replied Arahath Anuruddha.

Then, Samanera Sumana asked, "Alright Bhante, then may I leave right now to get you some water from Lake Anavatapta?"

"Are you sure you are able to do that, Sumana?" asked Arahath Anuruddha. "Of course I can, Bhante," replied Samanera Sumana.

Sumana the Novice Monk

"But make sure you keep this in mind, Sumana. The Lake Anavatapta is guarded and protected by a cobra named 'Panthaka.' He is the owner of that lake. But if you tell him that the water is needed for medication then he won't refuse to give you some," said Arahath Anuruddha.

Arahath Anuruddha cautioned Samanera Sumana in this way and gave permission to bring water from Lake Anavatapta.

Even though Samanera Sumana was only seven years old, he had amazing supernatural powers. It was a result of the merits he collected in his previous lives. Arahath Samanera Sumana worshipped Arahath Anuruddha and rose up into the sky and disappeared into the air to get water.

That day the Cobra King, Panthaka, was at Lake Anavatapta along with several others who had come to swim there. He saw the young monk coming towards Lake Anavatapta through the air.

"This novice monk is trying to put dirt on my head," thought the Cobra King angrily. He approached Samanera Sumana and asked furiously, "Why did you come here?"

"I came to fetch some water from Lake Anavatapta," replied Samanera Sumana. Just then, the Cobra King created a huge hood that fully covered Lake Anavatapta and said, "No, I am not going to give you any water. If you can find a way to get water, then you may take some."

Then, Samanera Sumana patiently said, "Please don't be angry, Cobra King. I came all this way to get some water because my teacher is sick and the only medication to cure his illness is some water from this lake."

"Monk, what are you talking about? Is there water only in my lake? There's water in the River Ganga as well. If you want you can take as much water as you need from there," replied Cobra Panthaka.

Again, Samanera Sumana pleaded, "Oh Cobra King, my teacher is suffering from a severe stomachache. He is in so much pain. He will only recover if he drinks some water from Lake Anavatapta. So please! Give me some water." But the Cobra King did not change his mind.

He said, "Novice monk, I'm sure that you have a lot of special powers. And I'm very happy for you for that. But you cannot take even a drop of water from here because I don't want to give you any. If you can somehow find any water, then you may take some," said the Cobra King unhappily.

Arahath Samanera Sumana got an idea as to how he could defeat the king and get some water. So he asked, "Alright Cobra King, can I take some water from here even if it is against your wish?" The Cobra King replied: "Of course! But try and see if you can."

Sumana the Novice Monk

Then, Samanera Sumana thought, "I shouldn't take this water without anyone knowing about it. I should let the whole world know about the power of the Supreme Buddha's dispensation while taking this water." By this time even Brahmas from Brahma worlds and Deities from Divine worlds were watching this incident. They talked among themselves: "Today at Lake Anavatapta we will see a great battle between two powerful beings." But some deities thought, "Oh, never mind the battle. All we want to know is who wins and who loses." They gathered around in the sky to watch the battle.

Since the Cobra King had said, 'If you have the power then you may take some water,' Samanera Sumana quickly squeezed the hood of the cobra and dipped it into the water. Just then, a huge stream of water squirted up into the air. Standing on the hood of the Cobra, Samanera Sumana filled his pot with water.

Devas and Brahmas saw this incredible achievement of Samanera Sumana and became extremely happy. With delight they exclaimed, "Sadhu! Sadhu! Sadhu!" When the Cobra King, who lost to the novice monk heard this sound he was very embarrassed. He became even angrier with the novice monk.

Meanwhile, having filled the water pot, Samanera Sumana rose up into the air and went straight to his teacher,

Arahath Anuruddha and said, "Bhante, here's the water, please drink some."

Sumana the Novice Monk

The Cobra King who was overwhelmed by embarrassment chased after novice bhikkhu Sumana but could not catch him. So, the Cobra King went to Arahath Anuruddha and said, "Oh Bhante, this novice monk harassed and embarrassed me and took water from my lake without my permission. So it is not right for you to drink this water." Then, Arahath Anuruddha asked Samanera Sumana, "Sumana, is this Cobra King telling the truth?"Sumana the Novice

In reply, Samanera Sumana said, "Oh Bhante, this Cobra King told me the most inappropriate things when I went there asking for water. He said, if we want water then we had better get it from River Ganga because he will never give us water from Lake Anavatapta. I asked him two or three times and each time he said 'If you can somehow find any water then you may take some.' Since he said that, I filled the pot with water and came. But I did not steal the water. He is telling a lie. It is not wrong for you to drink this water, Bhante. Please drink some."

Knowing that an Arahath bhikkhu would never lie, Arahath Anuruddha drank the water. As a result, he recovered from his illness. Then, Arahath Anuruddha turned to the Cobra King and said, "Oh Cobra King, this Samanera Sumana maybe very young, but he is very powerful. You can't even come close to his powerfulness. If you have a mind of hatred towards this novice monk then you must let go of it at once and ask for forgiveness."

Sumana the Novice Monk

Upon hearing the advice of this great Arahath, the Cobra King's hatred disappeared. He worshipped Arahath Samanera Sumana and asked for his forgiveness. Then the Cobra King said to Samanera Sumana, "From now on, if you need water from my lake then don't trouble yourself, just send me a message and I'll be happy to deliver the water to you." Having made this promise, the Cobra King went back to Lake Anavatapta.

During this time, the Supreme Buddha was staying at Purvārāma which was built by the famous lay devotee Visākā. So along with Samanera Sumana, Arahath Anuruddha went to see their great teacher.

Among the monks who resided at Purvārāma, one bhikkhu came forward and took Arahath Anuruddha's alms bowl and robes with respect. One novice monk there took Samanera Sumana by his hand and shook his head playfully thinking that he is just a novice monk. That novice monk did not know the powers of Arahath Samanera Sumana. He asked, "Oh little Novice, how are you? Are you happy with your monkhood? Can you sleep well at night without having dinner?" In this way, they asked pointless questions without allowing the Samanera Sumana to take any rest.

Sumana the Novice Monk

The Supreme Buddha saw this with His divine eye and thought, "The way those novices treated Sumana is not right. They do not know the powers of young Arahath Sumana. I must make all monks realize his power to prevent them from treating him this way in the future."

At that time, Arahath Anuruddha approached the Supreme Buddha and having worshipped the Blessed One, sat to aside.

While the Supreme Buddha was engaging in a Dhamma discussion with Arahath Anuruddha, the Blessed One addressed Bhikkhu Ananda: "Ananda, I wish to wash my feet with water from the Lake Anavatapta. Give the novice monks some pots and ask them to bring some water from there," said the Supreme Buddha. Bhikkhu Ananda called and gathered five hundred novice monks together.

Among them was Samanera Sumana. Bhikkhu Ananda lined up the novice monks in order and called upon the first monk in line: "Novice monk, the Blessed One wishes to wash his feet with water from Lake Anavatapta. Can you please bring some water from there in this pot." But the novice monk replied, "I am sorry, I cannot do that, Bhante," and refused to bring water. Then, Bhikkhu Ananda asked the second monk. The second monk's reply was the same. In this way, one by one, Bhikkhu Ananda asked the novice monks there. But all of them refused to bring water from Lake Anavatapta.

Sumana the Novice Monk

Finally, it was the turn of the last novice in the line, Samanera Sumana. "How can you refuse to bring water if the water is needed for our Great Teacher? I will bring some water from Lake Anavatapta," said Samanera Sumana. He received permission from the Supreme Buddha. Then, having worshipped the Blessed One, he carried the golden pot in his hands and rose high into the sky, disappearing into the air. The owner of Lake Anavatapta, Cobra King Panthaka saw the novice monk coming from a distance. Having recognized the young monk the Cobra King went forward and took the pot from Samanera Sumana. He filled the pot with water and said, "Oh Bhante, you can go ahead. I will carry the water pot and follow you behind." "No, Cobra King. Since the water is for the Supreme Buddha, I myself should take it. You can stay behind," replied Samanera Sumana. Having stopped the Cobra King, Samanera Sumana carried the pot himself, rose up into the sky and returned to Purvārāma.

From a distance, the Supreme Buddha saw the way Samanera Sumana was coming back through the sky and addressed the rest of the monks: "Oh Monks, just look at the way Samanera Sumana is bringing back water from Lake Anavatapta. It is astonishing! He looks just like a golden swan glowing in the air." Arahath Samanera Sumana put the water pot aside and worshipped the Supreme Buddha. With the intention of emphasizing the great power of Samanera Sumana, the Supreme Buddha asked, "Sumana, how old are you?" "Oh

Bhante, I am seven years old," replied Samanera Sumana. Then, the Supreme Buddha addressed the monks and said, "Oh Monks, this Samanera Sumana maybe the youngest here, but he is much greater in his powers. I have seen many trainee monks, but never a trainee monk who has such great powers."

So dear sons and daughters, take a look at the great powers of young monk Sumana, the great Arahath. Even someone as young as you has the ability to achieve great results. So you too must learn to practice the five precepts and develop good qualities within you. That's how this mind becomes pure. What a purified mind can do is unimaginable. Samanera Sumana was able to do all those great things because he took refuge in the Noble Triple Gem and purified his mind. Doesn't that show us the great power of the Triple Gem? If you too take refuge in the Noble Triple Gem then the benefit you will gain from it cannot be expressed in words. So my dearest children, you must take refuge in the Noble Triple Gem and try to practice the five precepts. The benefits you will gain from it are endless, just as they were for Samanera Sumana.

- The end -

Mahamegha English Publications

Sutta Translations
Stories of Sakka, Lord of Gods: Sakka Saṁyutta
Stories of Great Gods: Brahma Saṁyutta
Stories of Heavenly Mansions: Vimānavatthu
Stories of Ghosts: Petavatthu
The Voice of Enlightened Monks: Theragāthā

Dhamma Books
The Wise Shall Realize

Children's Picture Books
The Life of the Buddha for Children
Chaththa Manawaka
Sumana the Novice Monk
Stingy Kosiya of Town Sakkara
Kisagothami
Kali the She-Devil
Ayuwaddana Kumaraya
Sumana the Florist
Sirigutta and Garahadinna
The Banker Anāthapiṇḍika

To order, go to www.mahamevnawa.lk

www.ingramcontent.com/pod-product-compliance
Lightning Source LLC
Chambersburg PA
CBHW041235040426

42444CB00002B/171